D1GIT

Copyright © 2016 by Dr. Nathan Unruh
ISBN: 978-1-945255-01-4

All rights reserved. No part of this book may be reproduced or transmitted in any form or by any means, electronic or mechanical, including photocopying, recording, or by any information storage and retrieval system, without permission in writing from the copyright owner.

For information on distribution rights, royalties, derivative works or licensing opportunities on behalf of this content or work, please contact the publisher at the address below. Printed in the United States of America. Although the author and publisher have made every effort to ensure that the information and advice in this book was correct and accurate at press time, the author and publisher do not assume and hereby disclaim any liability to any party for any loss, damage, or disruption caused from acting upon the information in this book or by errors or omissions, whether such errors or omissions result from negligence, accident, or any other cause.

COMPANIES, ORGANIZATIONS, INSTITUTIONS, AND INDUSTRY PUBLICATIONS: Quantity discounts are available on bulk purchases of this book for reselling, educational purposes, subscription incentives, gifts, sponsorship, or fundraising. Special books or book excerpts can also be created to fit specific needs such as private labeling with your logo on the cover and a message from a VIP printed inside.

Book design by Tim Murray, paperbackdesign.com/books
Text set primarily in Minion, by Robert Slimbach

Throne Publishing Group 2329 N Career Ave. #215
Sioux Falls, SD 57107

D1GIT

One number that can transform your life

DR. NATHAN UNRUH

I have written this book to help educate you on how to live the life you want and deserve. It is my hope that this book will help you bridge the gap from where you currently are in your life to where you want to be, to see yourself the way God sees you, and to love others as you learn to love yourself.

I want to dedicate this book to YOU! I wish for you a transformational experience that will spread throughout your life, family, community, and ultimately, the world.

Contents

INTRODUCTION
1

LIVING YOUR D1GIT
5

YOUR SPIRITUAL D1GIT
21

YOUR MENTAL D1GIT
29

YOUR FAMILY D1GIT
43

YOUR SOCIAL D1GIT
51

YOUR CAREER D1GIT
61

YOUR FINANCIAL D1GIT
73

YOUR PHYSICAL D1GIT
83

PROGRESS, NOT PERFECTION
93

INTRODUCTION

Numbers.

Can you imagine life without them?

Ponder this for a moment. Almost everything you do, every day, is impacted by our numeric system.

Numbers were originally invented to track quantities and eventually to measure things.

Simple, right?

But now, thanks to numbers we can erect buildings, tell time, and build bridges. Numbers helped expand our world and numbers changed everything.

Numbers can change your life in just the same way.

Throughout this book, I am going to ask you to assign a single *digit*, that will rank the quality of results you are both getting now and you want to achieve in each area of your life.

Those digits will serve you in two ways: you will determine where you are and where (and who) you want to be.

We live in a world of movement, busy-ness and most often the illusion of progress. In all this activity, we can buy into the deception that we are making progress, but in reality, we may be no farther than we were a year ago.

We can avoid this deception by first examining and reflecting on the results we are getting. By quantifying the quality of our current reality. A ranking of results. A digit.

To get to where we are going, we must first know where we are.

We will put down the most important digit. The one that represents where you want to be.

But, be forewarned, the moment you choose your digit, you must absolutely commit to achieving it.

If you do this, I am convinced this digit will become the one number that can change your life. Permanently.

Thank you for the honor of reading my book.

Let's begin.

If you don't know yourself, you will easily be swayed from your purpose.

1
LIVING YOUR D1GIT

Living on purpose is about knowing what gets you out of bed in the morning, what truly inspires you, and what you love. When you are living on purpose, you never say, "Thank God it's Friday," you gladly say, "Thank God it's Monday!"

Your purpose should be authentic in order to keep you focused. Your purpose needs to be something that you are working toward that never drains your energy. When you are living a purpose-driven life, the end of the day has you feeling excited, not worn down. It puts a spring in your step, a glow on your face, and a twinkle in your eye. Your purpose makes you magnetic.

You automatically become emotionally charged each and every day when living on purpose, because you're serving something bigger than yourself. You don't get caught up in mundane conversations like, "My boss is a moron," "My coworkers are incompetent," and "This place is not taking care of us!"

Instead, you live an energized life. People who live on purpose have direction and intention. They don't wander through life as slaves of their circumstances; they create the right circumstances and environment to propel them closer to their vision.

Think of all the great leaders you have read about, or all the timeless victory stories we all remember. These people didn't succeed because of their circumstances, but rather, despite them. They beat the odds time and time again, and just when it seemed like they lost all hope, they got back up and took one more step, and you can do the same.

DEVELOPING SELF

To enter a stage of life where you are aware of your purpose, you must be involved in constant self-improvement. Start by taking a look at each area of your life outlined in each of the following chapters, and decide on a plan of action for improving each area.

If you are constantly improving each of these areas, you are improving your true self, and as you improve your true self, your corner of the world becomes a better place to live. You will become magnetic to good things and good people, and your life will be a magnificent trip.

WHO AM I?

If you don't know yourself, you will easily be swayed from your purpose. In fact, more than likely, you won't have a purpose.

If you don't take time to define yourself, your belief systems will be just a conversation piece instead of a way to live. If you don't know who you are, that means you don't know where you are going, and therefore, any road will get you there.

When you take the time to get to know yourself, you start paying attention to what inspires you and what appeals to you emotionally. You will then understand where you want to go and what path you need to take in order to get there.

HOW DO I FIGURE OUT WHO I AM?

I suggest you sit quietly and quantify where you are and simply take time to think. You must first know where you are in order to identify where to start. This will start the process of discovering your true self. Start by quantifying your wellness in each area of your life as you navigate throughout this book.

Always keep in mind that you are already "someone." Whether you like it or not, you have been the product of your environment from the day you were born. To figure out who you are, you've got to answer the questions of the seven spokes and ask, "Who have I become, and am I happy with the results? Am I happy with my health, my social wellness, my family wellness, and the other areas of my life?"

Whatever results you are getting in your life, they are primarily because of your actions, and your actions are being constantly motivated by your belief systems. We all have a belief system that has been ingrained within us through our experiences. It is important for us to understand that belief system before trying to make changes. Belief systems are difficult to change, but if we are committed to changing toxic and destructive mind-sets, we can soar to a whole new level of success and wellness. For this reason, I am asking you to look at present and past results. This will help you to identify your beliefs, and once you have done this, you will be able to change them to harmonize with your purpose.

Think about the environment in which you grew up. Were the people surrounding you generally positive or negative? How did they take care of their bodies? How did they manage their finances? As you consider this, be aware of the fact that you are an extension of that energy.

> *Whoever you are, there is some younger person who thinks you are perfect. There is some work that will never be done if you don't do it. There is someone who would miss you if you were gone. There is a place that you alone can fill.*
> —Jacob M. Braude

Your results are due in large part to the habits that were taught to you as you were raised. Assess if you have what you need to accomplish your purpose. Do you have the skills, the work habits, and the discipline that will be required to fulfill your purpose? Once you have done this, you will be able to see the changes you need to make, and the habits that you need to stop.

You may have people in your family who are or have been alcoholics, or were always broke. This does not mean that you have to be broke or that you have to be an alcoholic and repeat the cycle. You are not your parents. You can become fully aware of habitual family lines and make sure they end with you.

You must not allow any room in your mind for excuses. You can't say that you deserve more solely because you've had such a hard upbringing or don't ever catch any breaks. You are not your past and you are not your present circumstances. Your current results are nothing more than the sum total of your past thoughts and actions. You can change your future by deciding to change your thoughts and actions starting today.

Take the resources that I cover in this book, and begin to make thought-out action steps that include some accountability. This is how almost every successful person creates a life the way he or she chooses.

What goes unaccounted for does not get done.

One thing you have to remember about accountability is that the most important person who keeps you accountable is you! If you are passionate and clear about your purpose, you will want to be accountable to the action steps that you have set in place. Nearly every top-level executive has a trainer, every great performer has a team of expert advisors, and every world-class athlete has a coach; yet, many people go through their lives without anyone to help them achieve their potential.

> *Where I was born and where and how I have lived is unimportant. It is what I have done with where I have been that should be of interest.*
> —*Georgia O'Keeffe*

WHO DO YOU WANT TO BE?
Questions like "Who am I?" and "What do I want with my life?" can be molded together. You may even be able to start the process of self-discovery by asking, "What do I want?" before anything else.

I have found that when I ask someone what they want to do with their lives, they usually begin by telling me all the things they do not want. This is common because, initially, the results you don't want in your life will be much clearer than the results you do want.

If you are realizing unwanted results in your life, you don't have to accept them. As I said previously, as your thoughts and actions change, your results will eventually follow. For example, you don't want divorce in your family, so what actions can you take right away to create a loving, harmonious, and happy family life? You don't want to be overweight any longer, so what action steps can you take today to create new, healthier patterns tomorrow instead of falling back into bad habits?

Your answers to these questions will help you create a plan of action that you believe in.

SELF-IMAGE LIST

A great exercise for defining who you want to become is making a list of people whom you admire. Write down around seven to ten names, and really put some energy into this list.

Once you have the people selected, ask yourself why you admire them. What are the results they are getting that you want to manifest in your life? It is very important for you to recognize what you admire about these individuals because this will allow you to identify what you truly value in a personality and in a lifestyle. As you become clearer about your values and bring your actions into harmony with them, you will experience fulfillment. Below are some questions you can ask yourself to identify what you value and admire about the people on your list.

Perhaps you admire them based on the following criteria:

- Family time invested
- Commitment level to family
- Social life

- Marriage relationship
- Physical wellbeing
- Exercise habits
- Eating habits
- Dressing style
- Business success
- Financial success
- Service to others

Considering these aspects will give you a clearer picture and allow you to visualize the way you want to be. Can you see how powerful this is?

The more you live in harmony with your values, the more fulfilling your life becomes.

It is the visualization that is critical here. Visualizing gives you more clarity about where you are going and how you will get there.

This creates the ultimate litmus test. When you have a definite purpose, you can consider whether each action or behavior that you are about to take will move you toward your purpose or take you away from your purpose. Then, you can decide which action to take. What will you sacrifice? Will you sacrifice your dream and continue down the path that will not lead to your purpose, or will you sacrifice your comfort zone and move forward toward fulfillment? Either way, you must make a sacrifice.

GROWING YOURSELF

Spend time growing your true self, and then your professional and personal life will flourish! This is a natural effect of improving one's self. We have been taught by scripture to "seek first His kingdom and His righteousness, and all these things will be added unto you" (Matthew 6:33). One way to apply this lesson is to stop looking for something outside of yourself for your potential; your potential is within!

There is no potential in a college degree, there is no potential in owning a business, there is no potential in climbing the corporate ladder to presidential status, and there is no potential in investing in the stock market or real estate. There is no potential in any of these things because they are outside of you; all the potential that exists is inside of you.

You must work on yourself, but take care not to become selfish. By growing yourself, you must take into account the giving of yourself to others. Give of yourself in order to grow yourself. In times of giving, you have some of the largest gains internally. There is something truly special that happens within your soul when you give, and the greatest way to give is to give of yourself.

> *When a man has put a limit on what he will do,*
> *he has put a limit on what he can do.*
> —*Charles M. Schwab*

AUTHENTICITY

If this book teaches anything, it's to just be you. When you show up as somebody else, your power diminishes. Showing up as someone else displays a lack of being an *anchor* in your own belief system. When you are not anchored in your belief system, you cannot be effective.

Once you are comfortable in your own skin, your level of achievement and your level of fulfillment will improve exponentially. There is a tremendous difference between being respected and being liked. We all know people who change who they are in an attempt to fit in, people who try to be liked by everyone, but are ultimately respected by no one. This is a battle for many people. We are taught and conditioned to act a certain way in certain environments. When you are in church, you should talk this way, look a certain way, and act a certain way. Other social settings require other sets of behavior.

Here's a question: Why don't we act the way we do when we are with our best friend all the time? Why would we want to change our true selves for anything or anyone? God created you to be exactly who you are, and exactly where you are right in this very moment. Every single thing that has ever happened throughout your entire life happened exactly when it was supposed to happen to mold you into the person you are today. If you have become great, you have the choice to rise to a new level of greatness; if you have not become the person you intended, then you have the choice to begin again. All things can be made new for you and it starts with changing the very foundation of your belief system – your identity.

When you are locked into your true identity, you are an anchor. No matter who you are around or what environment you are in, you are anchored. You are who you are, no matter who's looking.

The more comfortable you are being your true self, the more vibrant, loving, and charismatic you become. Being an anchor is ultimately about becoming more confident and being yourself no matter what environment you are in.

> *Throw your heart over the fence and the rest will follow.*
>
> —*Norman Vincent Peale*

When you can do this, it means you are comfortable in your own skin. It means you have clarity about what the meaning of your life is. You are clear about your belief system and your purpose. You are living life with direction and focus. You are stable and certain in hard times and remain strong no matter what the circumstances. You are free from the need to be accepted, free from the fear of saying something you shouldn't, or free from the fear of acting in a way you shouldn't. This is being an anchor, and is an achievement in and of itself.

SELF-EXPECTATIONS

I believe the choice to be excellent begins with aligning your thoughts and words with the intention to require more from yourself.
—*Oprah Winfrey*

Self-expectations give you direction. If you want to accomplish a certain goal, then you have to take the appropriate actions, and your actions must match your ambitions. If you want to consistently perform at a certain level, your expectations need to be directly related to your actions, and your actions will be directed by your expectations. Shoot for the moon, and even if you miss, you will land among the stars!

If you expect to be successful in getting rid of twenty-five pounds, then your actions must begin with eating correctly, getting enough exercise, and so forth. In order to establish high expectations in your own mind, you must be totally clear about the expectations you are going to set.

The lower your expectations for yourself, the less of a reward you will receive. Your level of success in any area of your life is directly proportional to your expectations. Your expectations need to support your purpose. As you harmonize your expectations with your purpose, and your actions with your expectations, amazing things will start to manifest in your life.

Luck is when preparedness meets opportunity.
                                        —*Earl Nightingale*

High expectations and harmonious actions allow you to prepare to receive the good you desire. When something bad happens and you are not prepared to handle it, it is a very bad situation. There is something much worse, however, and that is when something absolutely wonderful happens to you, but you are not ready to receive it, and thus, you lose it. Be sure to prepare to receive the good you desire.

I mean exactly this: If you want to attract the perfect spouse, start becoming the perfect spouse. If you want to become a millionaire, start managing your money like a millionaire. If you want the perfect career position, start growing from your current position. If you want to be treated wonderfully by other people, start treating other people exactly how you want to be treated.

You know how the wind, no matter how blustery, remains as silent as it is invisible until it meets with leaves, and kites, and flags, and such? Well, it's exactly the same with the manifesting forces that make dreams come true until they meet with expectation. And right this second, they're whirling all around you.

                                        —*Mike Dooley*

START TODAY!
Only you can decide what your purpose is. When you clearly understand this, you can awaken each morning to possibilities rather than excuses. It's not what you do, but how you feel while doing it. If you lack energy and passion anywhere in your life, you lack purpose. Follow my advice in this chapter, and start to truly live.

> *Cherish all your happy moments: they make a fine cushion for old age.*
> —*Christopher Morley*

CHAPTER QUESTIONS
1. In this area of your life, what is your current digit on a scale of 1-10 with 1 being the worst and 10 being the absolute best?

2. What do you want your digit to be?

3. What is the first action you will take in order to take one step closer to your digit?

4. Who will hold you accountable to following through?

You are made in the image of God; therefore, you are important to the world and to the great work God is creating.

2
YOUR SPIRITUAL D1GIT

If I could pick any single belief to impress upon you in regards to your spiritual wellness, one single belief that would stay in your heart forever, eternally penetrating your mind, and undeniably giving you emotional peace, it would be that *you are forgiven*. You and every human being on this planet are unequivocally, unconditionally, and eternally forgiven.

Jesus paid the ultimate price for every single one of us. God sent his only son to die on the cross for our sins. This is the ultimate sacrifice. This is absolute commitment and full expression of the love of God for all humanity.

Rest your heart on the fact that no matter what you do or what you've done, Jesus has already paid that price for you. This sacrifice allows us all to inherit the kingdom of heaven. Our only role is to accept Christ as our Savior, repent for our sins, and stay obedient to a relationship with Christ through the wonderful peaks and treacherous valleys of life. Christianity is not a list of to-do's, it is a list of to-done's.

This is the majesty of grace. You have never done, nor will you ever do, anything to deserve such a reward; it is given to you by grace and through faith.

Knowing this gives you true *liberty*. You will have a sense of freedom that is truly indescribable when you accept this truth and integrate it with your behavior. The monkey can be permanently removed from your back. It is unfathomable how someone could love us when we may have done all types of negative and shameful things. All those rotten thoughts and actions can build a pressure in our heart. This feeling disappears once we accept the fact that those things do not matter anymore. The price has been paid by Jesus, and through Christ, we are forgiven.

Now that you have realized this, you are empowered and committed to having your focus directed toward Him. Your clarity, purpose, and focus becomes more in tune and intense.

> *"Come now, let us reason together," says the Lord. "Though your sins are like scarlet, they shall be as white as snow; though they are red as crimson, they shall be like wool."*
>
> —*Isaiah 1:18*

YOU ARE MADE IN THE IMAGE OF GOD

You are made in the image of God; therefore, you are important to the world and to the great work God is creating. Have you ever thought about the implications of this truth? I mean, really tried to wrap your mind around the undeniable fact that you are created, right now, in this moment, in the image and the likeness of God?

As you ponder this fact, it opens you up to the unlimited possibilities you have laid out before you. You not only begin to look at yourself in drastically different ways, but you also begin to look at the entire world differently. Your small dreams and problems will be thoughts of the past. In turn, you will open yourself up to receive all the abundance that is available for you to render positive service to humanity.

Humble yourself to God, accept that Jesus is your Lord and Savior, ask for forgiveness, dedicate your life toward advancing the kingdom, and your life will never be the same again—you will start to become aware that you really *are* created in his image.

Before I delve into this further, I want you to know that Christians aren't perfect. Christianity often receives criticism because people point to all the hypocrites that are within the church when, in fact, every one of us is a hypocrite in some way, shape, or form. Every one of us has his or her own demons or issues; that is part of being human—no one is perfect.

Below you will find what I refer to as the "Triple A."

This very simple, but powerful concept will allow you to strengthen your spiritual number! Remember that in order to receive eternal life it is not a matter of what you do, but what has already been done for you when Jesus went to the cross for each and every one of us.

TRIPLE A
1. Admit
First, admit your sins to God. Admit that you have been far from perfect—that you have fallen infinitely short of His glory. Through prayer, confess those things you know you have done wrong. Do not fear you will be rejected. Simply come to God and admit your vast need for Him, because we all need Him: His forgiveness, His strength, His love, His guidance, and His work in our lives. It comes down to this: being autonomous, independent, free-agent-type people will destroy us over time!! Admit to God that you have *not* trusted Him, and confess that you *want* to.

2. Accept
Secondly, accept Jesus—God's beloved Son, whom He sent to this world—as *your* Savior. We need more than someone to merely show us the right way (though Jesus certainly does that); what we need is a Savior to be our way, to be our salvation. That's Jesus. Accept his total and absolute forgiveness of your sins. He has promised to forgive all our trespasses when we trust in his life, death, and resurrection. He will *blot* them out—remove them

from us as far as the east is from the west. Accept this. Do not work to clean yourself up first; He will clean you up and rework your life from the inside out. Just come to Jesus in faith and you will find that all you need is found in him. His love is vast, and his mercy never-ending. Accept this.

3. Aspire

You have admitted you need him. You have accepted him anew. Now, aspire to be *like* Him. Let the grace of Jesus begin to transform the way you live every day. This is not about perfection; it's about progress. Ask *Him* to strengthen you to become like Him—because you will certainly not do it alone.

Truthfully, we will never be as morally righteous as Jesus (he was God!), but through his work in our lives, we can begin to look a lot more like Him, to love like Him. So, learn about his life. Get to know Jesus in a real and personal way. I challenge you to take up your Bible and read Jesus' famous Sermon on the Mount once a day for thirty days. See how this changes the way you view the gospel, your life, and the world. Oh, yes, it will challenge you, but I am convinced it will revolutionize the way you live, for the better. As we aspire to be more like Jesus you will find the strength, direction, and desire to improve all aspects of your life.

As you begin every day, go through these three points: Admit. Accept. Aspire.

THE BEGINNERS MIND

Everything that you've learned in this chapter as well as in this entire book was designed to be a beginning point for you. There will never be an end to your learning and studying. I want to urge you to continue studying this chapter, this book, and many other books on a daily basis. With each new idea, you allow new possibilities into your life. Every time you gain understanding, you gain strength and discipline.

A beginner's mind starts each day with remembering that *I don't know everything*. This attitude will expand your possibilities, lead you to new solutions and give you an air of humility that will draw people in.

I also encourage you to read the Bible every day. No matter how many times you've already read it or read a certain section, approach it with a beginner's mind. Remember, it is the written Word of God; the meaning contained in these words is infinite— you never *get* it, you only become more aware of how true it is. The more you let the truth of the Word sink into your mind, the more you become the person you were intended to become in your short stay on this planet.

Make sure you also talk to God on a daily basis. Do this as often as possible. You don't need to be in any particular location to have a conversation with God. All that is required of you is to be open to receive wisdom and to remain willing to act upon the wisdom that you receive. Talk to God like He is your best friend, because He really is. He is your truest friend on Earth. Do not feel as if you must speak with great words or specially designed repetitions, or that you even need to be clear on exactly what you want to discuss— just be open and willing.

Even though these habits will be hard to sustain and build upon, the reward is worth the effort. Your reward is eternity. Remain strong, steadfast, and obedient to the Word of God, and you will be given access to the kingdom.

As your world changes—which it will—do not keep it a secret. As you seek to know God, let Him be known to everyone you talk to. Make sure your friends and family know what has happened within you. Doing this gives them the opportunity to share your experience.

CHAPTER QUESTIONS

1. In this area of your life, what is your current digit on a scale of 1-10 with 1 being the worst and 10 being the absolute best?

2. What do you want your digit to be?

3. What is the first action you will take in order to take one step closer to your digit?

4. Who will hold you accountable to following through?

You must verbalize
the path you want
to take in life. Once
you verbalize it,
you have made a
commitment.

3
YOUR MENTAL D1GIT

If you study the lives of all the greatest successes, mental giants, and leaders of industry who have ever lived, you will find that they all have something in common. There is a golden thread that runs through their lives. They didn't become successful by luck; their success occurred as the result of specific principles and actions.

There is one truth that all of these high achievers firmly believed in. That great truth is the following: we become what we think about. The results in our lives mirror our most dominant thoughts. If you are thinking about poverty, that is what you will become. If your thoughts are directed toward prosperity, you will become prosperous.

This may seem far-fetched, but I can assure

you it is true. The thoughts you think cause you to feel the way you feel. Your feelings are expressed in the actions you take, and your actions produce your results.

This is the ultimate cycle:
1. Thoughts
2. Feelings
3. Actions
4. Results

To gain discipline, you must discipline your thoughts. To gain control over your actions and results, you must gain control over your thoughts. The first step toward gaining this control is through the proper use of affirmations.

AFFIRMATIONS

My definition of an affirmation is a personal declaration of a specific result you want to manifest in your life. It is a positive statement from yourself, to yourself. Affirmations are otherwise known as internal self-talk. If you observe your thinking, you will notice that you constantly make affirmations throughout your day.

Take a moment to write down some of the affirmations or statements you make during your day, and you will find that those affirmations match up almost perfectly with the results you are getting in your life. Affirmations are important because you must verbalize the path you want to take in life. Once you verbalize it, you have made a commitment. *Until you verbalize it, you are not truly committed.*

The next step, for now, is to create a list of affirmations. Understand that this initial list of affirmations will expand and evolve over time as you expand and grow. Don't be afraid to change or alter them as you move along; if they don't strike your emotions, they will have no effect on your behavior or your results.

Here are some action steps for creating a list of powerful, moving, and exciting affirmations:

Get a pen and paper, or open up a file on your computer, and do these following steps:

1. Make a list of every area of your life according to the seven spokes of wellness: spiritual, mental, physical, family, career, finances, and social.

2. Take each area of your life, and make a statement that clearly describes how you want to live in that particular area. Make sure it is only one or two sentences long. For example, let's say that you want to make an affirmation for health, and you want to be at your ideal weight of 150 pounds. Here is an example for your affirmation:

> *"I am so happy and grateful now that I feel healthy, vibrant, and alive at my perfect weight of 150 pounds."*

3. Make an irrevocable decision that you will execute behavior patterns that are in harmony with all of your

actions on the affirmations you have just made. If you made an affirmation similar to the one above for health, you will base all of your health-related decisions on the affirmation. If you have a choice throughout the day to eat a nice chef's salad or a caramel roll, base the decision on the affirmation, and stick with the salad; you'll be glad you did. I promise you, there is no food on the planet that tastes better than feeling healthy and vibrant.
Feel free to use someone else's affirmations as a template for your own until you get the hang of it. Remember, we are not shooting for perfection here, just progress. When you look at other people's affirmations, this will give you a good idea of how to formulate your own affirmations.

It is vitally important for you to understand these affirmations must stir your emotions. If they do not strike you emotionally, they will not have any lasting impact on your development. Emotion is the language of your subconscious mind. Emotion drives all of your actions, whether you understand that fully or not. This entire world is run on emotions. As you begin to declare these affirmations, you will find that you have greater control over your emotions as well.

You must fully commit to these affirmations. Be decisive and integrate your affirmations with your behaviors. If you want to earn more money, begin to learn about new avenues to acquire and earn wealth. Begin to develop or discover some marketable skill sets or talents that you have. If your affirmation for your family is, "I am so happy and grateful now that I have a perfectly balanced, loving, harmonious, and happy family life," then find more time to be with the most important people in your life. Tell them just how important they are to you. Express your love for them, and open yourself up to receive love back from them. Work on being fully present when you are spending time with your children.

I suggest that you make these affirmations in a way that will actually remind you of what is top priority in your life—what you want to be remembered for long after you have passed on from this physical world. Remind yourself of your commitment to God, and how your spouse and children are the most important people in your entire life. As you continue to remind yourself every day about what is important to you, you will find it much easier to make and keep your commitments to them. You will become more conscious of your decisions, and become aware of new opportunities that will allow you to spend more time with your family. This is a wonderful process, and it will make you feel more alive and fulfilled.

All of your affirmations should be in the present tense, not future tense, and they should start with two very powerful words: "I am." Your subconscious mind knows no time or place—only now. If you ask your mind, "Where am I?" or "What time is it?" it will always give you the same answer: "You are here. It is now." Knowing this, it becomes clear that all of your affirmations should be stated as if they are currently happening.

Do not say "I will" or "someday" or "I'm going to." Only say, "I am," and then take action as though you've already reached this state of being or goal.

Your affirmations should only include the positives. Your mind cannot focus on the reverse of an idea. If I tell you not to think of a purple cow, what image comes into your mind? A purple cow, right?

If you want to make an affirmation to help you quit smoking, do not say, "I am so happy and grateful now that I have quit smoking." Instead, say, "I am so happy and grateful now that I only take things into my body that make me feel vibrant, healthy, and alive."

If you want to get out of debt, do not say, "I am so happy and grateful now that I am debt-free." In that affirmation, you are focused on debt, and it doesn't matter if it increases or decreases. If you focus on debt, then debt is what you will create in your life. Instead, state, "I am so happy and grateful now that I am financially free!" Can you tell the difference? The first affirmation is focused on debt; the second is focused on financial freedom. Notice how you feel when you affirm these statements, and you can begin to see just how powerful these affirmations are.

THE POWER OF THE PAUSE
The power of the pause comes from silent time spent alone in thought and prayer. This is where you just be

still and be in the power of the pause. It is a time of renewal, sharpened clarity, increased focus, and strength. As we do this, we take the time to slow down, think and dwell on our mental digit. It's like a vacation for your mind, where you let go of worry, even if only for a few moments. You release any feelings of frustration, and get away from the constant noise of the world.

The clearer you are on what it is that you want, the easier it will be to reach the target. The more you are in stillness, the clearer you will be about what you want from your life, and what you want to bring to life.

Imagine a pheasant hunter intently walking through a patch of land with his dog. As the dog tracks down a nice pheasant and scares it out of hiding, what is the first action the hunter takes after he sees the bird? He aims, of course. He takes aim at the target, and the clearer the view he has of that target, the easier the shot. If the bird flies into a nearby shelterbelt, the hunter will have a difficult time getting a shot off, let alone an accurate shot; however, if the bird takes off and flies in clear sight for even a couple of seconds, it probably becomes dinner.

You see, the clearer the view you have of your goal (your digit), the easier it will be for you to attain it. The power of the pause allows you to aim at the number you want to hit. If you don't take the time to pause, it's like trying to shoot the target with your gun in the holster, or as the bird flies into the shelterbelt—it just won't work.

I recommend you find a spot where you are comfortable in order to do this effectively. Find a place where you will be uninterrupted, where you can dedicate yourself solely to the moment and the pause.

There is no right or wrong amount of time for you to spend doing this exercise. You can do it for sixty seconds, ten minutes, or an entire hour. If you are just beginning, first try to still your mind for a couple minutes at a time.

Begin the process by focusing on your digit, goals or affirmations. Be still, and read them to yourself out loud. It is important to do this aloud because this way you actually hear yourself declaring them. It stirs up your emotions and builds desire. Your mind will likely wander in the beginning, so verbalizing your intentions will prevent you from skipping around mentally and not truly focusing. The more physical senses you get involved with your affirmations and visualizations, the more of an impact they will have.

The more clarity you have on the goals you want to reach, the easier it will be to focus. This is where your digit will empower you to have a sharpened mind more than ever before. There will be no doubt in your mind what your target is, and that clarity will drive your affirmations, making them more powerful and concise.

Stating your affirmations aloud in the mirror will feel a little silly—maybe just plain weird—at first, but it will allow you to see the passion in your expression as you say these things. The affirmations will have a great emotional impact, you will develop more clarity, and it will spark new levels of confidence as you do this. I have a laminated copy of my affirmations in my car, and I read them before I go into the office each day. I also have a copy next to my bed, and I have them saved as a shortcut on my desktop. I place them in so many places to remind myself what I am working toward every minute of each day.

Another activity you can do during the power of the pause is writing or journaling. A goal is only an idea until it goes on paper. The same is true for affirmations. Writing them down will cement the idea and give it more form. The more commitment, the more clarity—and the more action you will be inspired to take.

How many of us have seen the two buddies sitting on barstools, talking about all the great ideas that they failed to act upon? No action results in no physical manifestation. Your actions must match your ambitions.

You can enter into the power of the pause anytime you please. Experiment with this to see what times of the day work best for you to be still. It is different for everyone; there is no right or wrong time. For some, the best time will be in the morning, to renew before the day starts. For others, it may be at the end of the day, to reflect and ask powerful questions such as, "What did I do that I am proud of or not proud of?"; "What conversations did I have that will help reinforce my stated purpose, affirmations, and goals?"; and "What is my recommitment to improving on my goals?" Find what works best for you, and make the power of the pause a habit.

GOAL SETTING

Earl Nightingale said that a person without a goal is like a ship without a rudder, subject to every shift of wind and tide. It is vitally important that you have specific and thought-out goals for your life.

Imagine a ship at sea that experienced an unfortunate encounter, and, as a result, one of the engine's stopped working, but the other engine on the other side of the boat continued to work causing the boat to shift off course. . Think about how that ship would just go around in circles, back and forth, shifting this way and that, until it finally ran out of fuel. It expended all its energy, and was very active, but ultimately went nowhere. Now, imagine the ship's engine props were all fully functional and working together. The ship could go wherever it had the physical capability to navigate. The captain of the ship could set an exact course, choose a specific port to dock at, and even estimate the travel time. The journey would be much easier, much less stressful, and more fulfilling for everyone on the ship.

Notice how both ships expended the same amount of energy, fuel, on their respective journeys. The only difference was that the second ship had all of its energy working in harmony toward a specific end point. You can see my point here. If we don't have goals, it becomes very easy for us to let our circumstances be our master instead of the other way around. We can control, to a very large extent, the quality of our circumstances, but we can never claim this divinely assigned power if we don't have goals.

Goals are dreams with deadlines. A great goal for yourself is one that excites you and is in harmony with your soul. It will be one of your reasons for getting out of bed in the morning. A good goal will give you something to hope for. An emotional goal will give you something for which to keep working and keep growing. It will give you a reason to get out of your comfort zone and live.

The most fundamental purpose of a goal is to give you the necessary incentive to grow in your awareness and understanding. Everything you have in your life is the expression of your current level of awareness, and one way to achieve more from your life, to be more fulfilled and prosperous, is to expand your awareness. This is why King Solomon said, "In all your getting, get understanding," or, in other words, awareness. Throughout the book of Proverbs, Solomon emphatically urges us to seek wisdom continuously, as though it were hidden gold and jewels, and I think he was right. After all, he was the richest and wisest man to ever live. The point is, if you don't have a good enough reason to grow or to get out of your comfort zone, then you won't. This is not because something is wrong with you; it is just the way you naturally are. We have been conditioned by the world to take the path of least resistance. We must give ourselves compelling, emotional reasons to grow instead of just maintaining the way we are currently living.

Everything in the entire universe is constantly in a

state of creation or disintegration. We are either growing, or we are dying. We are getting healthier or sicker. Every decision we make either takes us closer to our dreams, or pulls us farther away. The path that takes us backward toward disintegration is almost always the path of least resistance, so we must have a strong reason to move forward through our doubts and fears and into the life we want. As we keep doing this, it will become a habit, and our new, natural way of *being*.

Don't be afraid if things seem difficult in the beginning. That's only the initial impression.

> *The important thing is not to retreat; you have to master yourself.*
>
> —Olga Korbut

Keep moving forward, keep stretching, keep getting uncomfortable—this is good.

The main action to apply from this chapter is to simply take the time to think. Shut down from the world momentarily each day and the world of possibilities will expand beyond anything you have ever imagined! Create a new pattern of thinking! At first it will be uncomfortable, but the process is critical for you to progress forward in your life! Keep in mind that fear and discomfort are signs of growth and progress. One day, you will lift your head and realize how much you have changed. You will realize how enormously positive the impact of having the discipline to take time to just think has on you and those around you!

CHAPTER QUESTIONS

1. In this area of your life, what is your current digit on a scale of 1-10 with 1 being the worst and 10 being the absolute best?

2. What do you want your digit to be?

3. What is the first action you will take in order to take one step closer to your digit?

4. Who will hold you accountable to following through?

We must continually strive to put family first in a world where we are demanded to move in many different directions...

4
YOUR FAMILY D1GIT

Even though you may be out trying to make a living and provide for your family, spending quality time with them will remind you why you are living. It is not about the quantity of time you spend with them as much as the quality of time you spend with them.

While we try to teach our children all about life, our children teach us what life is all about.

A lot of people think that just because they are at home in front of the TV, they are spending time with their family. I want to make a suggestion right away for this chapter, and that suggestion is to do a "media fast" with your family. Shut off the TV; in fact, cancel cable. Who needs it anyway? Stop calling it the TV, and start calling it the Automatic Intelligence Reducer.

Think about who you want to be with when you are at the final stages of your life. Who do you want around your bed when you are ready to drift off into eternity? Not your coworkers or joint venture partners. Not the stars you watch on TV. You would want the most important people in your life to be right there with you—your family.

This is a simple truth we must try to remember. We must continually strive to put family first in a world where many things demand we move in many different directions according to what trend is cool, what friends and coworkers want to do after work, and what is expected of us in different social environments. There are many distractions from our success and from our family time as well.

If you haven't been spending time with your children when you know you should, realize that you can change that right now. You change that the moment you make the decision that you are going to change.

Make a written commitment to yourself, to your family, and to God that you are going to put the first things first in your life.

> *What you leave behind is not what is engraved in stone monuments, but what is woven into the lives of others.*
>
> —*Pericles*

Be aware that, just as with your business success, when you make decisions and commit to those decisions, the universe will help you in many different ways to manifest that goal. So, let's approach this like any other goal. You must start by being exact about what you want to do. What is the end result that you want? Develop a clear mental picture. Make it big, beautiful, and absolutely overflowing with love and joy.

Visualize yourself living and experiencing the kind of love and family time you want with your family. See yourself and your children expressing yourselves boldly and truthfully, holding nothing back. See everyone in your family fully expressing the love you have for each other. See everyone making the time to do fun activities and create memories that will last for eternity.

> *Children spell love... T-I-M-E.*
> —*Dr. Anthony P. Witham*

Will creating this picture and scheduling more time be tough for you to do? Absolutely! Again, we all have demanding schedules and expectations that we have to live up to. The change may be a quite radical change in the beginning. It will require total commitment and persistence. Where there is no way, a way will be made, but you must be totally committed.

There will be days when it will seem easy, and maybe even more profitable, to take time away from your family and spend it doing other activities. You will be tempted to compromise, but do not give in. Remember, your family is one of your highest values, and the more you show them respect, the more you demonstrate your total commitment to them through your actions, and the more confident you will be in yourself.

The more you operate in harmony with your values, the more self-esteem you will gain. The more self-esteem you gain, the more success you will have in life. And the more success you have, the more time you will be able to spend with your family. It is a wonderful cycle.

I will say it again. You must remain totally committed. Continually commit to this family time and the goals for your family time that you just established. Think about it: you want to make your family time something wonderful, and so does God. You are not alone in this. This will be the best investment of your entire life. Time with your family is an eternal investment. You will always be able to look back on this time you spent with them, and no one and nothing will be able to take it away. It will stand for all time.

You can lose money overnight, your business can burn to the ground in a matter of hours, and your car can be leveled by a dump truck in the parking lot, but when you spend an afternoon with your family doing what brings you all joy, at the end of that day that time stands for eternity. You will always have that memory. You will always be able to say that, on that day, you put the first things first. You kept the main thing the main thing. Here are some actions and ideas to help you make the most of the time you have with your family:

CREATE A FAMILY NIGHT

Select one night per week when you will do nothing but spend time with your family. This solution is simple and easy to do. Get creative, and make a theme for each night, such as movie night, takeout night, game night, or pizza night. Have fun with it, and make it something that your entire family can participate in.

Don't forget to let your guard down and just *talk*. Just relax, kick back, and talk with your children. Communicate free from judgment or the need to tell them what you think they need to be doing. Just talk with them, and stay in rapport with love—just love.

LET YOUR CHILDREN DECIDE

Many parents try to force their values and dreams on their children. This will surely create conflict and resistance to your input as the child grows. If they select an activity to sign up for and decide it is not for them, let them make that choice. The more you help guide your children into making decisions for themselves, the more they will be open to your input and guidance. This may seem counterintuitive to how we are supposed to be as parents, but it will work for you.

Let them explore their passions at an early age. Let them decide on the movie, the dinner, or maybe even the clothing they wear. Choose your battles. As you do this, you give your child one of the greatest skills in the world: the skill of decision-making.

ENGAGE IN OUTSIDE ACTIVITIES
Go out and enjoy nature with your children. The more you encourage them to be active, the more active they will become. Active children are healthy children. Help them form the habit of activity rather than lounging.

This will give you an excellent opportunity to teach your children how to love themselves, others, and the planet. You can teach them to appreciate the gift of having the earth as one massive playground for them and everyone else around them.

READ WITH THEM
A family who grows intellectually together grows closer together. Select books, Bibles, and/or devotional guides that your children will enjoy reading. Whatever subjects they are interested in, find reading materials in harmony with their passions. A great way to spend quality of time with your children as well as cultivate a yearning to read and learn is to intentionally make time to visit your local library as a family.

FAMILY PROJECTS
Create projects or activities that involve the entire family, whether you go to a basketball game, play cards, or do something very simple. Our family enjoys sporting activities and therefore I intentionally will find ways that we can all attend sporting events as a family. We enjoy the energy, competition, conversations, and just the overall

experience that helps to strengthen our relationships.

The bottom line is to engage. Engage your spouse, and engage your children, and to do that, you must engage yourself. Sometimes, we can take the most important people in our life for granted! The best way to avoid taking those we love for granted is to be in a state of gratitude for each and every day. Gratitude will prevent you from taking anyone or anything for granted. Start with gratitude in your heart and pour yourself out to your family. Engage and be thankful.

CHAPTER QUESTIONS

1. In this area of your life, what is your current digit on a scale of 1-10 with 1 being the worst and 10 being the absolute best?

2. What do you want your digit to be?

3. What is the first action you will take in order to take one step closer to your digit?

4. Who will hold you accountable to following through?

The people you surround yourself with will either be the greatest allies for your success, or the worst enemies.

5
YOUR SOCIAL D1GIT

Social wellness involves connecting and networking with people who share your belief system. When devising a plan of social wellness, it is important to think about what kind of person you want to become, and then find people or groups with whom you can interact and allow your values to be expressed in your life. If you want to be a better mom or dad, hang out with people who are good moms and dads. If you want to make more money, network and nurture relationships with people who have achieved or are achieving financial wellness.

Carl, manager of the Manager Foundation, said that environment is more important than heredity. He believed that the people we surround ourselves with have more of an impact on our overall wellness than the genes that we inherited when we were born. That is a pretty powerful observation, and one I agree with wholeheartedly.

Think of the people you hang around with most often in your life. They may be your closest friends, coworkers, members of your church, or your family. Think about how they live their lives for a moment: their family life, the quality of their relationships, and the depth of their bank account. As you do this, realize that, statistically speaking, you are likely within ten percent (more or less) of their results. In other words, your income is roughly within ten percent of their income. The amount of love you experience in your relationships and the number of pounds you are over or underweight are all more than likely within ten percent of their results.

This evidence of the power of our environment demands that you become more aware of what results your closest friends are getting. The people you surround yourself with will either be the greatest allies for your success, or the worst enemies.

Do not look upon others with judgment, but rather with awareness and love. Observe their behaviors, and if they are not acting in harmony with your values, then you must reconsider the time you spend with them. I am not telling you to completely abandon them, just don't spend as much time with them. This will be a tough decision on your part, but it is one you must make.

SOCIAL WELLNESS STARTS WITH SERVING OTHERS

Does it feel better to give or to receive? The most successful people I know understand that when they serve others they get the most out of life and find a true sense of satisfaction. I am talking here about true giving—giving without any expectation of return. Just like anything, your intentions count the most. Am I talking about giving your talents, money, or time? Yes and no; all of them and none of them.

You see, true giving is a way of being. It is the spirit in which you live and think. When your first question is "How much can I give?" instead of "How much can I receive?" you embody infinite wisdom and experience financial opulence.

Giving can involve your talents, money, and time. It can also involve none of those things. You can give the greatest gift you have—your attention—to someone and change his or her entire day, week, or even life.

Give yourself to someone who could never pay you back. Give your time to someone who may not be grateful for the blessing you just bestowed on him or her. Give your knowledge to someone who may not respect it.

When you give, you don't focus on what you are going to get; you are giving for the basic feeling and experience that as you give, you are expanding possibilities for all humanity. As you give, you create, and as you create, you expand the kingdom of heaven.

MAKE SOME NEW FRIENDS

Join a civic group or participate in a service organization that resonates with your belief system. This will help you align your actions with your values. When your actions are in alignment with your values, you will radiate fulfillment and joy, which ultimately attracts new and positive people into your life.

Reconnecting with an old friend can be a wonderful experience. It will not only allow you to reminisce, but it will also serve as a reminder of where you came from and how much you have grown. Connecting with old friends can be a breath of fresh air, and a relaxing retreat down memory lane. Do this as often as possible, and you will have relationships that last a lifetime.

Join a church, and become active. By joining a church, you will be able to reconnect with what may be your long-lost friend as well—God. Reconnecting with God will bring incredible feelings of newness and love on all subjects. When you are a member of a church, you are about a higher purpose. You are part of a group of people who are united by a common belief, which will make it easier for you to meet new people.

Meeting new people is scary to some. It is not always comfortable to be in a new environment where you don't know anybody. One way to help overcome this fear is to start to understand people better.

We all have a tendency to judge others based on a multitude of factors, most of which are false and unfair preconceptions. Instead of being judgmental, become more curious. To become more curious, ask more questions. Through questions, we start to understand other individuals. As we become more curious about others, we deepen and strengthen relationships. People don't care about how much we know until they know how much we care.

SEE A COUNSELOR

Many times, our behaviors have become so engrained in us that it is difficult to break old habits that are destructive toward our social wellness. I encourage people to visit a counselor who can help uncover those destructive patterns and plan action steps to remove them. Choose a counselor who resonates with your belief systems and who challenges you to live a better life.

Working through family issues, personal issues, and the damage done to us by others with a professional who can see our issues more objectively and give us proven strategies for coping and moving forward is a vital component of transforming your social digit.

PERSONAL DECLARATIONS

All conversations are fundamentally an exchange of energy or emotions. Have you ever been around someone who was full of smiles and compliments, but you just didn't feel right around that person? Or maybe you met someone who made you feel immediately comfortable even though you didn't know very much about him or her? This is an example of how we give off energy or feelings to other people. This happens via molecules from your subconscious mind to another's subconscious mind.

You can charge your body to have a positive and magnetic energy. One way to do this is by verbally declaring the state of being you want to embody. For example, if you want to give someone positive feelings of joy and encouragement, you would repeat these declarations out loud:

I am in overflow.

All is well and joyful.

I radiate happiness and gratitude. I am healthy, vibrant, and alive.

Don't wish you were in a better mood – declare the mood you want to experience and live it out!

RID YOUR LIFE OF TOXIC RELATIONSHIPS

As I mentioned earlier in this chapter, if you truly want to live with passion and purpose, it is vital that you rid your life of toxic relationships. I define toxic relationships as any type of relationship that does not promote your life purpose. For example, let's say you truly feel called to be a division one girls' basketball coach. Whenever you talk about coaching, if all that your friend can focus on is why you can't do it, why you aren't good enough, or why it will be too hard for you, then he or she needs to go. This doesn't mean you completely shut off all contact with them; just don't see them as often, and don't stay as long.

Whenever you're in conflict with someone, there is one factor that can make the difference between damaging your relationship and deepening it. That factor is attitude.

—*Timothy Bentley*

There will be some people in your life you will continue to love unconditionally, but you just won't spend as much time with them as you have in the past. You won't be attached to what they do or say, but you won't judge them, and you will understand that they are doing the best they can with the awareness they have.

There is a fine line here. I want to be clear that just because you choose not to interact with them as often doesn't mean you stop loving them. God has given everyone free will, and people make their own decisions based on their personal beliefs.

This is how Jesus taught us to love and be in relationships. He did not hate the other people; He compassionately loved them while choosing to live in a different way. You see, the fact that you've made this decision today doesn't mean that another person is bad or less than you; it just means you are willing to accept people for who they are. You love them; you just don't participate in any destructive activities. You changing your life could give them the motivation and inspiration to make the changes for themselves.

Embrace and love yourself just the way you are. Embrace and love other people just the way they are, just as Christ did.

Social wellness is a state in which you are at ease in your environment, whether that is at work, or while participating in leisure activities. It involves developing relationships with other individuals through positive interactions in which feelings are communicated and expressed without fear of judgment or rejection.

Social wellness involves caring for others while allowing others to care for you. You need to schedule time to spend in activities that promote social wellness. These activities may be professional or leisure, depending on whether you are at ease within your environment. The main objective here is to be at peace, to be calm, and to be actively giving to others.

Studies show us that people who don't have social wellness are more susceptible to illness and have a death rate two to three times higher than those who are working to be socially well. Social wellness also enables you to adapt to stress more easily than those who isolate themselves.

Have you ever seen a person who has a strong social network? They are positive and have a high self-esteem. They are magnetic, and people want to be around them. They have an unending stream of opportunities and blessings are coming their way—this occurs because of their social movement. They are in the stream of good because they are socializing with other successful individuals.

Build your social network to support your belief system. Your social network is the strongest when you spend it with people who have the same values as yourself. Create your network deliberately to create meaningful, lasting relationships that will be both fulfilling and profitable to you and your family.

CHAPTER QUESTIONS
1. In this area of your life, what is your current digit on a scale of 1-10 with 1 being the worst and 10 being the absolute best?

2. What do you want your digit to be?

3. What is the first action you will take in order to take one step closer to your digit?

4. Who will hold you accountable to following through?

Work was made for us; we were not made for work.

6
YOUR CAREER D1GIT

What inspires you?

What energizes you?

What are your hobbies?

What would you gladly do for free?

Your answers to these questions will give you perfect guidance into what career, job, or business is right for you. It is important that you truly love what you do. If you don't, it will be very difficult to stay focused, motivated, and progressive throughout your days.

I strongly recommend you read *Now Discover Your Strengths* by Marcus Buckingham. As you harmonize your labor with your natural strengths, you will find your workdays are much more enjoyable.

Work is supposed to be fun! Work was made for us; we were not made for work. You were given talents and passions that no one has ever taught you, and it is through those latent talents and passions that you will find your life's work.

You will spend more time "working" than almost anything else in your life. The average person works over 150,000 hours in their lifetime. You will spend around forty percent of your waking hours working. In fact, it has been said that you will spend more time working, thinking about work, and commuting to and from work than eating, drinking, playing, and vacationing combined.

Stop and think about this for a moment. If you are going to spend forty percent of your waking hours doing something that is necessary for you, your family, and your life, then you should take as much time as you need to figure out what kind of work will bring joy and happiness into your life.

After all, if you don't love what you are doing, then you maybe missing out on your potential and a life lived that gives you fulfillment and impact. Time is one thing you can't control, and you can never get it back. This life is not a practice run—once you spend time on something, it will stand for eternity. Nothing can be done to change it, and you will never be able to go back.

This subject of work is serious business because you

are part of a much bigger picture. Remember when we were talking about living with purpose? A major way to do this is to align your work with your purpose and passion. Your chosen field of work will be the machine for manifesting your purpose on the physical plane we are living on for now.

You may be saying, "I know what I love, but I will never make any money at it!" Stop that thought process immediately, and don't worry about the money for now. I will show you the right way to earn money in the chapter entitled "Financial Wellness."

Besides, working is the worst way to earn money. Wealthy people don't make their fortunes solely through their own work. They leverage their time and earn their money through multiple sources of income. It is the money they are earning through the many different avenues that allows them to do the work they truly love.

WORK COMMITTED

Commit your work to the Lord, then it will succeed.
—Proverbs 16:3

The Bible tells us all our work will be fruitful and successful if we commit our work to God. When we are committed to our work and to a specific outcome, the universe will help us reach our goals every time.

There must be total commitment to your goals and work. If you allow the slightest amount of room in your mind to give up or put your goal on hold, you will not reach the target.

Listen to what Goethe says about commitment here:

Until one is committed, there is hesitancy, the chance to draw back—Concerning all acts of initiative (and creation), there is one elementary truth that ignorance of which kills countless ideas and splendid plans: that the moment one definitely commits oneself, then Providence moves too. All sorts of things occur to help one that would never otherwise have occurred. A whole stream of events issue from the decision, raising in one's favor all manner of unforeseen incidents and meetings and material assistance, which no man could have dreamed would have come his way. Whatever you can do, or dream you can do, begin it.

Boldness has genius, power, and magic in it.

Begin it now.

Notice how he explains that when we are truly committed, Providence moves too. This is a powerful quote here by Goethe and one I recommend you hang in a place where you will see it and read it often.

It is important not only to commit to your goals and your work, but you also to commit every day to the spirit in which you do your work. Are you going to give every single minute of this day your absolute best, or are you going to go through the motions like many people do?

Grab a pen and paper and create a written description of the attitude you will work in. This describes not what you will be doing, but the spirit in which you will be doing it: a spirit of dedication and commitment.

Work as if God created this position specifically for you. Work with the attitude that everything that you do today is an assignment from God himself. Do this, and watch the joy and glory of the Lord manifest with and through you each and every day.

> *Whatever you say or do, let it be an example of the Lord.*
>
> —*Colossians 3:17*

WORK WITH ENTHUSIASM

Enthusiasm is contagious. This is true of positive and of negative enthusiasm. Napoleon Hill said that if you place a person of high enthusiasm in a company, no matter how large the company, eventually that person will impact every single person in the company, whether positively or negatively.

When the ancients witnessed a person of enthusiasm, they believed God himself had touched the individual, guaranteeing them success in whatever endeavor he or she pursued. Talk about putting an enormous amount of value on enthusiasm!

Enthusiasm comes from the Greek word *enthous*, which means "inspired by God." When you are enthusiastic, you radiate a magnetic energy that attracts all that is good while drawing out all that is noble in you.

Your next question should be, "How do I get enthusiasm?"

If you do not currently have enthusiasm, understand that no one is born with it; it must be developed. You can develop enthusiasm by harmonizing two of your most powerful mental faculties: imagination and will. Your mental faculty of imagination is what allows you to build any picture you choose on the screen of your mind. Your will is the mental faculty that allows you to hold one idea on the screen of your mind regardless of what is happening around you.

Imagine anything you want, and your body reacts accordingly. If you imagine negative mental pictures, you will feel negative. If you imagine positive mental pictures, you will feel wonderful. So, the first step in developing enthusiasm is to harness the wild horses of your imagination. Instead of building negative mental pictures (i.e. worrying) and letting your imagination run wild, choose to deliberately build a mental picture of yourself already living your dreams. Harmonize your will with the mental image you have built. In other words, make a conscious choice every single day to give more energy to this new mental picture than any worry in your life. Build it up in your mind and focus on it with your will.

WORK HARD

> *"Go to the ant, you sluggard; consider its ways and be wise!"*
>
> —*Proverbs 6:6*

Here is a great ingredient to living the life you choose and having success and fulfillment in your chosen career: work hard. Be focused and relentless for the chosen set of hours you will labor.

When I talk of working hard, I do not mean being miserably exhausted or doing the things that you don't like to do all day. I mean giving every workday your absolute best, not stopping at a certain point because you don't get paid enough. I mean giving the company you work for or the business you are operating for your best possible performance each and every day.

As the proverb above states, consider the ant. Ant colonies are comprised of individuals working tirelessly to achieve a common goal in the best, most efficient way possible. They serve as nature's example of innovation, teamwork, and a tireless work ethic. Entomologists inform us that a single ant can lift ten, twenty, or even fifty times their own weight. If you consider their size, that's shocking. But as equally as shocking is the truth in this statement: Most people over-estimate the amount of work they can do in a day and under-estimate the amount of progress they can make in a decade. As you are working your daily grind, keep the big picture in mind.

Do this, and you will get slightly better every day. Even if you only improve one percent a day, which means in a year's time, you will have improved 365 percent overall. That adds up to a dramatically noticeable improvement.

Try to make everything you do during your workday about the expression of your soul. No matter how mundane the task, make it about the expression of your greater yet-to-be. If you are typing a report, how can you make it your very best? How can writing that report help you express your greatness? How can that simple report you have done hundreds of times actually help you evolve more and express your higher self? Your potential will begin to surface as you focus all your effort on fulfilling that objective to the absolute best of your ability.

Work hard and don't stop. You will surely have days when you don't feel like getting out of bed due to the mountain of tasks that await you, but don't quit. Don't surrender your leadership to outside circumstances. Keep moving forward at all times. Even when you come to a point where you don't know what to do next, just move forward. Action is always better than no action—you can do it!

Life is too short to waste. Dreams are fulfilled only through action, not through endless planning to take action.

—*David J. Schwartz*

WORK SMART

You must develop the work ethic to work hard and the awareness to work smart.

How can you leverage yourself more?

How can your work be duplicated by someone else?

How can you use the effort and money of other people who have the same vision and purpose as you do?

These are a few questions that should be thundering through your mind on a daily basis. If you seek true wealth and career success, you must leverage yourself—no exceptions.

Another secret to working smart is to always evaluate your performance. Consistently ask yourself, "What actions are working for me, and what actions are not getting results?" and then simply do more of what is working and less of what is not working. Keep it simple and profound.

> *A dull ax means harder work. Being wise will make it easier.*
>
> —*Ecclesiastes 10:10*

To end this chapter, I want to strongly recommend you read the book *The Energy Bus: 10 Rules to Fuel Your Life, Work, and Team with Positive Energy* by Jon Gordon. This book talks about how to fill your life with meaningful and inspiration accomplishments. Every person and company must learn how to overcome negative energy in order to operate at the highest level possible. This book will show you and your teams how to do just that.

CHAPTER QUESTIONS

1. In this area of your life, what is your current digit on a scale of 1-10 with 1 being the worst and 10 being the absolute best?

2. What do you want your digit to be?

3. What is the first action you will take in order to take one step closer to your digit?

4. Who will hold you accountable to following through?

When it comes to money...you don't get what you deserve. You get what you earn.

7

YOUR FINANCIAL D1GIT

"Work like you don't need the money, love like you've never been hurt, and dance like nobody's watching."

—*Anonymous*

WHAT IS MONEY?
The answer may seem obvious, but I want to kick off this chapter by putting money in its proper place. Money is energy. It's neither good nor bad – it's neutral. When you witness someone buying/selling something, you are observing an exchange of energy. You are watching an exchange of one service for another. Money is an exchange for services rendered.

Understanding this, you should never set a

goal to make money. The only people who make money are the ones who work in the mint. If you want more money, you must earn it.

Have you ever wondered why some people don't seem to work very hard, yet earn large amounts of money? At the same time, there are people who labor long, hard hours and seem to earn very little money. Why is this? It almost seems to be unfair; the hard worker deserves just as much money as anyone else. When it comes to money, however, you don't get what you deserve. You get what you earn.

So how do you earn more? I will share with you the exact law that governs how much money you, me, and every other person on the planet earns. It is the law of exchange. Understanding and applying this law in all of your business affairs will increase your income faster than any other factor you could learn about.

The law of exchange states that the amount of money you and I earn will always be in exact ratio to four factors:

1. The need for your service
2. Your ability to render your service
3. The difficulty to replace your level of service
4. The quantity of services rendered

Let's break these factors down. The first factor is the need for your service. There must be a demand for the service you are rendering or the product you are selling. It doesn't matter how good you are at selling a typewriter because there is no demand for them anymore. At one point in time, the need for a typewriter was huge, and people earned large amounts of money selling, creating, and repairing these products. Today, however, they are long gone.

You see the point? Your product or service must have a massive demand in today's marketplace. No demand will equate to no dollars.

We move to number two in this financial equation: your ability to render your service. There may be a huge demand for your service, but you must be very good at providing or selling that service. Your profession may be that of a wellness coach, a performing artist, or an accountant. Even though there is a large demand for these professional services, you must ask yourself, "How good am I at my profession?" You must be a master at your chosen profession in order to earn large amounts of money. As consumers we have many choices. Consumers demand results and results are created through mastery!

As you become very good at doing what you do, you will become very difficult to replace and automatically come into harmony with the third part of this equation.

It is very difficult to find a true professional in any industry. There are a lot of people working hard, a lot of people who call themselves professionals, but very few who have truly become difficult to replace due to their highly specialized levels of service.

*When a man has put a limit on what he will do,
he has put a limit on what he can do.*
—*Charles M. Schwab*

The select few who have mastered this part of the equation are not difficult to point out in a crowd. Their performance sticks out. They are good, they know they are good, and they know why they are good. They shine with confidence, assurance, and prosperity.

If you ask them why they are so successful, they may not be able to tell you the exact reasons; however, whether they know it or not, they are in total harmony with the law of exchange. Most people of wealth that I know and have observed become outstanding at providing a service in high demand.

*Let us not be satisfied with just giving money.
Money is not enough, money can be got, but they
need your hearts to love them. So, spread your love
everywhere you go.*

—*Mother Teresa*

They also provide their services to a large demographic of people. This is the fourth part of the equation, the quantity of the service. You must provide your service to as many consumers as possible without sacrificing quality.

You could have an excellent service or product, but you must distribute it to the largest number of people possible in order to earn high incomes. This is an obvious part of the equation, but it is important to understand this when you are making plans to distribute your service.

BE A GOOD STEWARD OF YOUR MONEY

In order to amass real wealth that will last, you must start by creating a monthly budget that you follow absolutely. However, the word budget carries a bit of a negative connotation with it. Therefore, instead of referring to it as a "budget" try thinking of it as a "profit plan". They mean the same thing but since the goal of your budget is to increase your profit let's focus on the positive! If you have never done this, don't worry. If you can do simple math, you can make a monthly profit plan.

I will now give you the basic steps you must follow to create a monthly profit plan. This example will only be for one person, but you can add or subtract the numbers as they are relevant to you.

The first step is to calculate the income you earn every month. If you are in an hourly or salary position, simply take your annual income, and divide that number by twelve.

Next, determine the necessary expenses that you must pay in order to live. I am talking about the payments you absolutely must pay to keep a roof over your head, food on the table, and survive.

In today's world these would be:
- mortgage/rent payments

- clothing
- groceries
- heating and electric bills
- car gas/maintenance/ payments
- cell phone payments

The third step is to take each of these expenses listed above and determine how much you spend monthly on each individual expense. Payments such as the rent/mortgage and car payments will remain constant. The others may fluctuate, however they should stay in relatively the same range.

In order to properly estimate these necessary expenses, take one month, and write down every single dollar you spend on the necessary expenses that may fluctuate such as clothing, groceries, heating/electric, gas, and car maintenance. This month will provide you with the most realistic expense expectation. Then bring out your bills and records from the last three months, factor in the fourth month (the one where you keep track of all expenses), and average them all together to give yourself a good baseline number to work with. Once you have the average of all four months, add between 5-10% so you have a cushion to work with. This number is the monthly cost of surviving.

Step number four will involve calculating all the non-essential expenses you accrue every month. Step three got us the cost of living on the bare minimums. However, you and I both know that this isn't how we want to live. Therefore we must calculate other expenses that add to the quality of life. These will be deemed " unnecessary expenses" because in all reality you can survive without them. Expenses such as eating out, Netflix, school expenses for kids and even after work recreation fall into this category. Once again keep track of all of these expenses in the same month that you calculate your necessary expenses. This may be an eye-opening experience that will allow you to determine where you can cut back on some unnecessary spending.

Determine what lifestyle is in your means, and allocate an amount of money for recreation. I want to caution you on this point: do not live beyond your means. There is good debt, and there is bad debt. Good debt is acquired through assets such as real estate or business loans. Bad debt is credit card debt used for anything other than emergencies.

> *The most powerful force in the universe is compound interest.*
>
> —*Albert Einstein*

Compounding interest is an amazing thing. When you acquire a lot of credit card debt, however, you can quickly get on the negative side of compound interest. Having bad debt like this hangs a burden over your head that can smother your true desires from coming to fruition.

Take your expenses and compare them to your income. Make every attempt to make your income exceed your expenses.

The greater your understanding of money, the better you will manage and invest the money you have. This will create a wonderful circulation of money into your life. The best material I have found for financial literacy is Dave Ramsey's Financial Peace University. You can visit his Web site at www.daveramsey.com. I personally recommend his book titled *The Total Money Makeover*. This book has all of his core teachings condensed, organized, and made practical. Dave also has a course available entitled *Financial Peace University*. You can search and join a group that could be happening in your local area and this course, just as his book, is highly recommended.

Another important concept I want to highlight is how important it is to give. The phrase "give and you shall receive" isn't only present multiple times throughout scripture, I can personally attest to seeing this phrase lived out in everyday life. Look at the most successful people you know, they aren't the ones that are pinching pennies and hoarding all their earnings for themselves. Often times they are the ones that are the most giving, not only of their money, but also their time. I often hear people complain about the concept of tithing and questioning why God wants their money. I agree with them, God doesn't want your money! He wants you! He just knows how closely money is tied to your heart!

Lastly, it is staggering how much free time and mental peace you will have when you don't have to worry about money. Learn how to use it, save it, and invest it so it will become a source of blessing instead of a source of frustration for you and your family.

CHAPTER QUESTIONS

1. In this area of your life, what is your current digit on a scale of 1-10 with 1 being the worst and 10 being the absolute best?

2. What do you want your digit to be?

3. What is the first action you will take in order to take one step closer to your digit?

4. Who will hold you accountable to following through?

No person or thing can take your health away from you if you decide to treat your body the way God intended you to treat it.

8
YOUR PHYSICAL D1GIT

The concept of "health" has been distorted throughout the years and the current healthcare system holds much of the responsibility for the distortion. The World Health Organization defines health as "a state of complete physical, mental, and social well-being and not merely the absence of disease or infirmity." The absence of sickness does not equate to being healthy! The absence of pain now doesn't mean you are living in an optimal state of health!

The muddying of the concept of health can be attributed in part to three very dangerous "half-truths". These half-truths have been propagated and developed into principles that have misguided all avenues of healthcare! I will briefly explain these three half-truths: The Gene

Theory, The Germ Theory, and the Stress Theory. The purpose of defining these three theories is to further expose the truth relating to your physical health. You are equipped with all the tools necessary to live a healthy life!

THE GENE THEORY

The Gene Theory states that all disease processes can be blamed on the genes that we inherit. Sadly, a 2011 study concluded that you are either born with the gene that likes Brussel Sprouts or you are not. It is this type of laughable pseudoscience that contributes to the public's confusion.

The full truth is that genetic mutations or bad genes can and do cause problems. What main stream science and research doesn't tell you is that less than 20% of diseases are caused by genetic mutation. That means that the knowledge establishing the Gene Theory does not contribute to the remaining 80% of diseases known to the human population. The remaining diseases are influenced by our environments. This portion of the theory is called epigenetics and helps add to the "whole truth."

The term epigenetics refers to the changes in gene expression that does not involve changes to the underlying DNA sequence. It is the science of how environmental signals select, modify, and regulate gene activity. This new awareness reveals that our genes are constantly being remodeled in response to life's experiences. These signals can be nerve signals, food molecules, toxins we ingest, stress hormones, the water we drink, and yes even our thoughts! Over time, adapting to our environment can actually result in physical changes to our bodies!

The addition of the field of epigenetics has increased the validity of the Gene Theory by proposing that external factors and our environment can induce physical changes to our health. However the thought process relating all diseases back to the genetic composition of a human is still the backbone of the Gene Theory and a great cause for concern as these ideas continue to shape how the general population views health!

THE GERM THEORY

The Germ Theory implies that many of our illnesses whether it be the common cold, flu or many of the infections that plague us are all caused by the microscopic underworld. The Germ Theory would have us believe that we are victims of the these tiny creatures that live in the air we breathe, the soil we walk upon, the countless surfaces we touch and yes, even the people we interact with. With this mindset, we are left defenseless because it is simply a matter of time before these critters invade our bodies and take over.

What the Germ Theory fails to leave out is that the research shows that bacterial cells outnumber human cells at a ratio of 10:1! Based on quantity alone we are left with very little chance of survival! By this ratio our bodies themselves are 90% bacteria and only 10% human.

We are at the merciless control of bacteria!

This fear based, victim of nature mindset leaves us with only one plan....kill all the bugs. Never thinking some are important and play crucial roles in maintaining the health of our bodies. Some bugs exist in the human body to clean up the garbage we leave behind with our poor diets and poor habits!

The truth is there are some strains of bacteria and viruses that are harmful to our bodies. However, where the Germ Theory leads the general population astray is with the fear-inducing thoughts designed to scare us into thinking we are in danger. The truth is that most of these strains have been created by living out of balance with nature, trauma, and the chronic overuse of antibiotics.

STRESS THEORY

We do live in a stressed out nation. A national poll done in 2014 by NPR, the Robert Wood Johnson Foundation, and the Harvard School of Public Health found that more than 1 in every 4 Americans say they had a great deal of stress in the previous month. Half of all adults say they experienced a major stressful event in the past year. This number works out to more than 115 million people!

The effects of stress are well-documented and not too hard to notice during an average day. When we are stressed we feel it in all aspects of our lives. The problem with stress is that there are so many different types of it: financial, personal relationships, family, home responsibilities, work, the list goes on and on!

The least discussed and potentially the most important type of stress is what is known as Eustress. Eustress is defined as beneficial stress. Learning new information or working out are two examples of activities that place stress on the body, good stress! Eustress helps us grow and rise to new levels which allow us to increase the levels of stress we can expose ourselves to.

Stress is not the problem. The inability to handle and deal with stress is! Just as humans have learned to harness the power of roaring rivers in order to power our daily lives; we need to learn to adapt to stress! Put a strategic plan in place to not become a victim of stress, but a victor.

NEUROVITALISM

Now that you've gotten a glimpse of the theories that have led to the distorted world view of health, we can begin to examine the real truth behind our bodies natural ability to heal. Neurovitalism is the idea that by maintaining and caring for your nervous system you allow your body to regulate itself the way it was designed to be self-regulated. You've been exposed to neurovitalism since you were a child; you scrape your knee and begin to bleed. Your body recognizes there is a problem, stops the bleeding, fixes the damage and returns your body back to its natural healthy state. The part of the healing process that is left out of this story is that all of the body's responses are coordinated by the components that make up the nervous system. If you believe that we have a central nervous system (which anyone with a brain should!), then you understand the general functions it performs. The brain sends signals to the nerves spread throughout the body. The major route of this signaling is right down the center of the body through the spinal cord. It can be thought of as simply as this — the brain controls all aspects of the body.

If you're reading this thinking "If the nervous system controls my body's ability to heal, what can I do to keep MY nervous system healthy?" then you are on the right track! Caring for your nervous system is only one part of caring for your overall health. Caring for your physical health is not a passive movement. It requires intentionality and living with a purpose that says "Nothing can stop me from improving myself." If you struggle with motivation in pursuing a healthier you, just look at your support team surrounding you. Imagine how much the lives of everyone around you will be improved by getting to deal with a healthier, happier you!

It might be easier to use the analogy of your health as a piggy bank. Every day you are either depositing or withdrawing from the piggy bank. If you continuously withdraw and take out money from the piggy bank without depositing anything back in what's going to happen? You end up broke! Your health is no different. If you continuously withdraw from your health in the form of eating food you shouldn't, excessively drinking, taking days off from exercise, etc., you will begin to see your health piggy bank become scarce. However, you are able to deposit and build up your health piggy bank by making good deposits such as exercising, eating right, controlling and overcoming stressful situations, or taking time to spend with your family. The more you are able to deposit, the better off you will be in the long run and the more you are able to withdraw without serious consequences. Just like your personal banking accounts, if you want your wealth to grow over the long run you have to deposit more than you withdraw. This is no different for your physical health!

Improving your physical health isn't something that you should focus on doing solely by yourself. Regardless of whether you are a strong self-motivator or not, it's much easier to take the hard road when you can make stops along the way! There are several different avenues that must be considered when improving your overall physical health. Thankfully, there are experts trained to help guide and support you through each avenue. If you want to make a lasting change to your physical health you should look into opening (or renewing) relationships with several different professionals. A chiropractor, massage therapist, nutritionist, personal trainer, dentist, medical physician, optometrist, acupuncturist, physical therapist, or yoga instructor will do nothing but benefit you as you strive to achieve your physical health goals!

As a chiropractor by trade I can speak to what we as a profession are able to do to help you achieve your health goals. Your chiropractor serves as your doctor of the nervous system. Chiropractors are trained to identify where nerve interferences exist in the body and to correct them to restore proper nerve flow. This allows for the proper connection between the brain and body. By removing these interferences the power is restored to all avenues of the body. When most people think of chiropractors, they think of neck and back pain, which chiropractic is very effective at treating! However, chiropractic is not just limited to these issues! I encourage you to meet with your local chiropractor and discuss how chiropractic can become a key component in helping you improve your overall physical health!

CHAPTER QUESTIONS

1. In this area of your life, what is your current digit on a scale of 1-10 with 1 being the worst and 10 being the absolute best?

2. What do you want your digit to be?

3. What is the first action you will take in order to take one step closer to your digit?

4. Who will hold you accountable to following through?

Whatever you do, do it with all your heart.

CONCLUSION: PROGRESS, NOT PERFECTION

Now we are at the end of your journey through this book, and hopefully you have taken a journey through your entire life. I hope that you have taken stock of exactly what results you want in your life today and what results you do not wish to experience anymore. I hope that you have thought deeply about the ideas contained in this book and have asked yourself the tough questions. I hope you have closely observed your daily actions, pinpointed the habits that will not serve you, and completely raised the *spirit* in which you do your new actions.

One of the most important points here is that wellness is a journey, not a destination. Wellness doesn't come in a pill, a potion, or a lotion. It is the constant strive for balance between all seven spokes.

Remember, the only way to get new ideas is to ask good questions. As long as you never stop asking yourself questions, you will never run out of ideas. As long as you remain fixated on the solution, the problem will never overwhelm you. As long as you keep making progress each and every day, no matter how big or small that progress may be, you will find yourself one day surrounded by the things, circumstances, and people you truly love.

So congratulations and thank you. You've finished reading this book, which puts you ahead of the 80%+ readers who start books and don't finish. While that statistic is alarming, I have to wonder how many of the people who do finish books just move on to the next book and do nothing.

If I could leave you with one final idea it would be to do something. Do anything, but please do something *that matters*!

Get in front of a whiteboard, write down the major action points you took away from the previous chapters, pick one and *do it*! And whatever you do, do it with all your heart.

You, me and everyone you see today will all reach our final hour. And if we have the gift of experiencing those last minutes of our life with our family, what is the legacy you are going to want to leave them with? Will there be anything left unsaid? Will there be anything left undone? If so, get it done. Your legacy starts today.